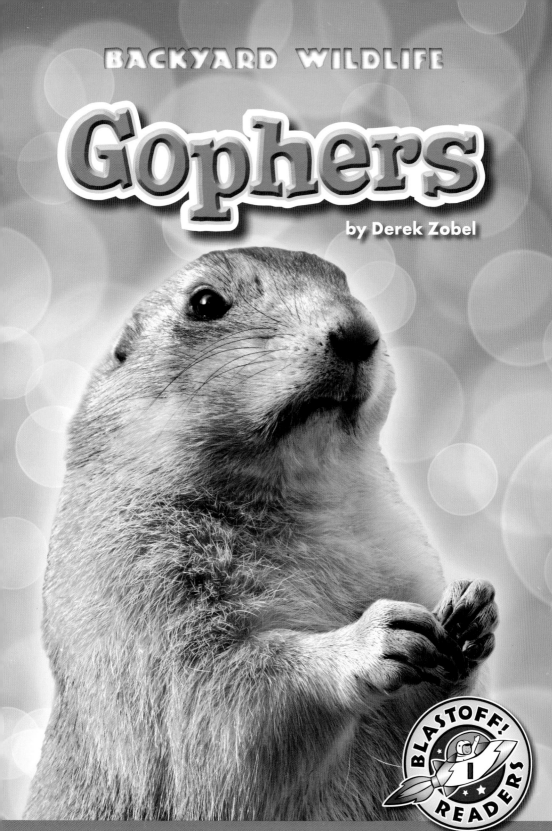

BACKYARD WILDLIFE

Gophers

by Derek Zobel

BELLWETHER MEDIA · MINNEAPOLIS, MN

Note to Librarians, Teachers, and Parents:

Blastoff! Readers are carefully developed by literacy experts and combine standards-based content with developmentally appropriate text.

Level 1 provides the most support through repetition of high-frequency words, light text, predictable sentence patterns, and strong visual support.

Level 2 offers early readers a bit more challenge through varied simple sentences, increased text load, and less repetition of high-frequency words.

Level 3 advances early-fluent readers toward fluency through increased text and concept load, less reliance on visuals, longer sentences, and more literary language.

Level 4 builds reading stamina by providing more text per page, increased use of punctuation, greater variation in sentence patterns, and increasingly challenging vocabulary.

Level 5 encourages children to move from "learning to read" to "reading to learn" by providing even more text, varied writing styles, and less familiar topics.

Whichever book is right for your reader, Blastoff! Readers are the perfect books to build confidence and encourage a love of reading that will last a lifetime!

This edition first published in 2012 by Bellwether Media, Inc.

No part of this publication may be reproduced in whole or in part without written permission of the publisher. For information regarding permission, write to Bellwether Media, Inc., Attention: Permissions Department, 5357 Penn Avenue South, Minneapolis, MN 55419.

Library of Congress Cataloging-in-Publication Data
Zobel, Derek, 1983-
 Gophers / by Derek Zobel.
   p. cm. – (Blastoff! readers. Backyard wildlife)
 Includes bibliographical references and index.
 Summary: "Developed by literacy experts for students in kindergarten through grade three, this book introduces gophers to young readers through leveled text and related photos"–Provided by publisher.
 ISBN 978-1-60014-597-1 (hardcover : alk. paper)
 1. Pocket gophers–Juvenile literature. I. Title.
 QL737.R654Z63 2012
 599.35'99–dc22

                                      2011002252

Printed in the United States of America, North Mankato, MN.

080111   1187

Contents

Gophers are **rodents** with brown and gray fur. They are also called ground squirrels.

Gophers have four long teeth. Their teeth never stop growing.

Gophers use their teeth to **gnaw** on food. They eat roots, fruits, nuts, and **insects**.

Gophers carry food in **pouches** in their cheeks. Their pouches can hold a lot of food.

Gophers bring the food back to their **burrows**. They store it there for later.

burrow

Gopher burrows
are also called
gopher towns.
They have
many tunnels.

Gopher towns are found in grasslands, hills, and mountains. Thousands of gophers can live in one town.

Gophers must watch out for **predators**. Hawks, badgers, and coyotes hunt gophers.

A gopher stands
guard near a
gopher town.
It **whistles** when
it sees a predator.
Get inside, gophers!

Glossary

burrows—holes in the ground that some animals dig; gophers live in burrows.

gnaw—to bite or nibble on something for a long time

insects—small animals with six legs and hard outer bodies; insect bodies are divided into three parts.

pouches—pockets some animals use to store food; gophers have pouches in their cheeks.

predators—animals that hunt other animals for food

rodents—animals that usually gnaw on their food

whistles—blows air through the mouth and lips to make a sound

To Learn More

AT THE LIBRARY

Baum, L. Frank. *The Discontented Gopher*. Pierre, S.D.: South Dakota State Historical Society Press, 2006.

Boldt, Mike. *The Gophers in Farmer Burrows' Field*. Tulsa, Okla.: Yorkshire Publishing Group, 2009.

Green, Jen. *Gophers*. Danbury, Conn.: Grolier, 2004.

ON THE WEB

Learning more about gophers is as easy as 1, 2, 3.

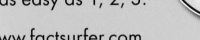

1. Go to www.factsurfer.com.

2. Enter "gophers" into the search box.

3. Click the "Surf" button and you will see a list of related Web sites.

With factsurfer.com, finding more information is just a click away.

Index

The images in this book are reproduced through the courtesy of: Steve Allen/Getty Images, front cover; Juan Martinez, pp. 5, 9 (right), 13, 15, 19 (middle); Bernd Zoller/Photolibrary, p. 7; Norbert Wu/Minden Pictures, p. 7 (small); Marco Tomasini, p. 9; Carlos Caetano, p. 9 (left); Martin Novak, p. 9 (middle); Curt and Cary Given/Photolibrary, p. 11; Mare Salerno, p. 13 (small); Laurie O'Keefe/Photo Researchers, Inc., p. 15 (small); Shin Yoshino/Getty Images, p. 17; Proehl Proehl/Photolibrary, p. 19; Henk Bentlage, p. 19 (left); Denis Pepin, p. 19 (right); Mark Tomalty/Masterfile, p. 21.